THE DAWNING OF TWENTY THREE

Keaton Mills

House of Grace

Copyright © 2024 Keaton Mills

All rights reserved

No part of this book may be reproduced, or stored in a retrieval system, or transmitted in any form or by any means, electronic, mechanical, photocopying, recording, or otherwise, without express written permission of the publisher.

ISBN-13: 979-8-9899437-0-8

Cover design by: Apphia Salter

Printed in the United States of America

CONTENTS

Title Page
Copyright
Preface
Walking 1
SEEK 3
Yellow 4
Blue Light 5
Mars 6
Responsibility 7
Tree of Hope 9
Checkpoints 10
Legendary Love 11
August 9 13
Emerge 14
One Day 16
While You Wait 17
Asking Questions Pt. 1 19
I'll Send You Flowers 20
Asking Questions Pt. 2 21
The Long Version 22
Did You Find Joy Today? 23

August 20	24
Lonely's Heartbeat	25
Dear Z	28
Fight Back Season	30
Meadow	31
Afterword	33
About The Author	35

PREFACE

This collection is dedicated to the year 23. That year brought many firsts in my life. It brought pain and sorrow. Grief and loneliness. And at the very end joy and relief. I loved hard that year but the intensity came with tough lessons that I wasn't ready to learn yet.

This collection was formed through words of wisdom friends, family and strangers gave to me in my 23rd year of life. It's my diary that gave me language for walking through what felt like my first 'true' year of adulthood. This collection is a reminder to myself and hopefully to you, that you earned the steps you are taking right now.

Let these words sit with you. Let them speak to your thoughts and when you are done, be sure to breathe.

With Love,
K.M.

WALKING

They say I'm only crawling
Not realizing that I've started walking
I don't mind the unsolicited advice
As long as they're not scoffing

At my inexperience,
Because "You're just a baby"
But if they had seen my grief lately
They'd be wondering how I get up daily

Fighting the whispers that merge themselves with my thoughts
While waging a war for all I had lost

But "You're just a baby"
So I hold my breath long enough for the unconsciousness to win
Praying that in my escape I find peace within
The gravity of your loss now becomes my physical existence
And if the pain would release my heart, I'd find you in the distance

But I'm just a baby
So I learned how to stand on my own
Because without your love I had to find a new definition of home
See in my inexperience, I have experience
With a grief that would make you delirious

They saw me crawl through shock
But didn't stay when denial had knocked
And my legs were still shaky when anger creeped in
And bargaining took my appetite so much it made me thin
Depression shook me to my core
Making me best friends with the tears on my floor

So after a year, I finally accepted that hope could be on the horizon
And took my first steps without over-correction

So I remind myself to eat now
Because I made you a vow
That I would learn how to walk on my own

So when my tears make my vision blurry

I'll get up, wipe them and here you say "Don't you worry"
See they say I'm only crawling
Not realizing that I had started walking

SEEK

The Divine loves to have a good "ki ki" with me
When I said yes to a journey of 40
I assumed that meant renewing
But it wouldn't be a journey without a few pits
So let me break it down a bit

Days 1 through 6 were euphoric
Feeling on top of the world, then there goes my logic
And before I knew it, my life became chaotic
See when grief comes, its' remains can become toxic

10 through 17 brought peace that was conflicting
And while I was overthinking
You reminded me that there was nothing I was missing

So I stepped into Your will
Put my pride to the side
And let obedience be my guide
But on day 20 You called my name
And told me to serve even through the pain

It wasn't the easiest task
But I realized You wanted me to observe instead
In my service, I found the common thread
In You being my daily bread

So I felt relief wash over on day 31
Because the breaking brought out the sun
Your word remained true
And the blessings You promised were now my virtues

Seeking You was the best journey I could be on
It taught me that the darkest days still have a dawn
And your love for me was the strong rock I could stand on

You wanted me to emerge
As the promise You spoke into the Earth
As the testimony of Your divine work

YELLOW

Your raspy voice held the warmth of my favorite cup of coffee
Topped with whipped cream
It was the sweetness in your caresses that lulled me to sleep
You gave me the biggest blessing my eyes had ever seen
The tenderness of your love gave me wings

You didn't restrain your love from us
It even came with a couple of licks
A couple of conversations laced with tough love
But I always felt your wisdom that was wrapped in your hugs

The lines in your hand held the lineage
of the cypress tree outside our home
Your presence brought the only sun that I've ever known
But I wasn't prepared for when God called you home

I still had questions to ask
About how my yellow came to be
About when you decided to combine red with green
And what it meant to fight to just to be free

I apologize for holding you too tightly
I never wanted to cause you pain
And you taught me that in sharing, I would always gain
Your love are where my roots remained

But my mosaic's version of yellow is partly dull
Because the peace You brought is now null and void
Leaving me in gray matter that left me paranoid

My rainbow hasn't been as full since you last exhaled
But I promise to try and love even still
And honor the yellow you left inside of me

BLUE LIGHT

It was 77 by the time I was 4
And while that could've been more,
I wasn't worried
By the time I could drive to the store
I had so many that would've started a world war
About me

And well...that shock wore off,
and I was filled to what I thought was my capacity
Until you came along changing my reality
With your warm southern hospitality
That made me believe in duality
Because you helped carry my tragedy masterfully

So when you said 'I hadn't met all the people
that were going to love me yet'
I had to take a moment and let that set
Because your love came without a debt
So when I pull out my palette to paint my mosaic of the word love
I'll be sure that your color brings the essence of a morning dove
Thank you for reminding me to expect love

So now I don't count how many people love me,
I let my love fly free
In hopes that it lands somewhere in the sea
As a forever thank you to my color blue: LT

MARS

"Do you believe wounds can heal?"
Well if I showed you a picture of space, would you believe it?
What if I showed you a picture of a spaceship?
You laughed and said "Why don't you get a grip?"
But while you were being smart at the lip
I'm trying to tell you why I didn't quit
See while my mind went to combat
My body held the bruises of an acrobat
Displaying them like a 5pm broadcast
And it left me without anyone to contact
So my wounds became my habitat

I wonder if I showed you a picture of Mars
Would you see the symbolism in our scars?
The impact from my trauma
Leaving a crater that erased any evidence of nirvana
I'm trying to tell you why I didn't quit

Because there was once life there
And the rushing sound of freedom filled the air
And if you cleared the dust that covers Mars
You'll see that the craters are reminiscent of my scars
They are reminders that rivers once flowed
And if I held on long enough, I could still see tomorrow
So that's why I didn't quit

Because if I show you my scars now
You'll believe wounds can heal
And the beauty behind Mars will finally be revealed
See Mars was my mirror…to everything I couldn't see
It shows me my past and the endless possibilities
Of what the future holds for me

So I put the pills down
Because what was lost had finally be found
So when you asked me
"Do you believe that wounds can heal?"
Do you see why I said "Yes, because Mars has some appeal"

RESPONSIBILITY

They say heavy is the head that wears the crown
But the load is heavier for those that He calls to breakdown the generational curses
that were sown into our family grounds

And I was beginning to think
That my prayers would sink
But these blessings came with new responsibilities

That when you're called to serve
You must leave ego at the door
Even as your faith is on floor

So I am letting go of the plans I made for me
Grieving what I thought would be
and letting gratitude be my attitude
Because these prayers went beyond what I could see

So now it's my responsibility to do the unthinkable
Remove the barriers that prevented me from trusting You
Because You've always had the bird's eye view

Loving me through all of my doubts
And letting me thrive even in a drought
Shifting my proximity to blessings
To see that You had given me new responsibilities
Which is my ability
To respond to the blessings You have for me
So I could rest in Your powerful divinity

So thank you for doing the work on the inside
Turning my grief into joy
And taking on my fights
To provide for my bloodline

There aren't enough words to express
The rest my soul has found
In how You've taught me to kill my flesh
So that my spirit was no longer bound

I release the pressures I assigned to myself

And take on the new responsibilities of this wealth
But I thank you for the lessons in the journey
And your continued favor and mercies

TREE OF HOPE

You reserve the right to feel your emotions
But you're also entitled to your healing

CHECKPOINTS

Don't look at it as a finish line
Look at it like checkpoints
Because this life has a way of making you second guess if it's really your time
And you'll lose yourself looking for a sign
Waiting for everything to align

So cry because it hurts
But don't let your thoughts make it worst
This time put on a shirt
And then listen for the word

Choose to brush your teeth this time
So maybe the day doesn't feel as long
And don't forget to turn on your favorite song
So you can see your thoughts were wrong all along

This moment has to release you after while
And Maya said every storm will run out of rain
So don't get used to this pain
Because life can bring the sweetness of a sugar cane

So give yourself grace for what you didn't know
And next time the seasons change
Take it as a sign that you're beginning to grow
Because the true healing begins tomorrow

LEGENDARY LOVE

When I think about how you love me
I get chills
Your presence administers the pills
that ease my pain
Your eyes remind me of the peace I feel after it rains
Yeah...your love is legendary

See when I think about how you love me
I am reminded of the depths of the sea
You know how more than 80% is unseen
somehow you miraculously discover new parts of me
Journeying to areas that have destined to be freed
Yeah...your love is legendary

The way you support without me asking
You're ready for the task understanding
That even on my bad days, you'll be clapping
Because you know what it took for me to just keep standing
Your love is legendary

The way you pour into my cup so delicately
Because you know you catch more flies with honey
But dishing out tough love
When you know my spirit has had enough
And always reminding me that this life is a journey
And I won't arrive just because I'm in a hurry
You wait for me
To understand that every good thing will always find me
Yeah...your love is legendary

And I'll never be able to repay
the kindness your heart has displayed
Enduring my attitude even on the darkest days
And the biggest blessing to date
Of mentioning my name even as you pray
Your love is legendary

And I hope that you know I don't take it for granted
That God gave me a gift I never imagined
In a person that doesn't see loving me as a challenge

And I promise to put all of the love you give me to good use
Never to accept someone's half assed love as an excuse
And standing strong in the virtues
that your seeds produced

And I promise to love without hesitancy
While applying all that you've taught me
About anyone coming to love me
They first need to provide proof of residency
Yeah…your love is legendary

So I hope that I can make you proud
Because the love you've given me has been profound
Everyone should experience legendary love
And let it hold them as their heart breaks
To remind them that love is still on the way
And their healing never arrives late

When I think about how you love me
I see a sanctuary
Because your love is legendary

AUGUST 9

Dear God,

It is a big thing, what you do everyday. I want to say thank you for the protection I can see and the divine grace that covers what I can't see. Whatever this next season is, prepare me to walk it out. May I have the discipline that sustains me to live in the freedoms you give. May Your virtues of love, kindness, compassion and patience be magnified in me that people experience You first in connecting with me.

In Jesus Name,
Amen.

EMERGE

It was hard to see you hurt
Because there was nothing I could do
From stopping the mess spill out
from stopping your heart from breaking
It was like watching the family china set break into a million pieces

Because you were always behind a glass covering,
You know for safe keeping
Until that year at thanksgiving
We only let family come into the house
So we trusted that each intention was pure
They smiled in our faces,
because our trust in them was verified by you
Otherwise we never would've let a stranger touch our family heirloom

I watched as you sat on the couch
Watching the formation of intricately stitched memories
They were always so delicate with you
So I didn't catch when your joys had turned to the blues
Because you said you were safe, behind the glass covering

I watched as they helped you dance through despair
Carefully planting seeds of the fruit you always wanted to bear
But I mistook the cracks in the china forming
As parts of the pattern of your beauty
And I missed the rhythm changing in your breathing
Because I thought you were safe behind the glass covering

So when dinner was ready, we let them set the table
Which was unusual because we didn't let strangers touch the china
But they had become an expert in how to care for your mind, body and soul
So we trusted a stranger with our family heirloom

And then the glass covering was opened
Releasing the pressure that was building
from all the moments that cut through your exterior
Leaving you vulnerable to your own interior

They took the first dish out and sat it on the table
Creating conversation that caused distraction
And then for the first time I noticed how they handled you without care
Your eyes pleading as if you knew they were never supposed to be there
But I trusted what you told me
How they listened to your heartbeat as their favorite record
Knowing how you felt about your day before you did

I trusted the joy behind your eyes
That even when it got rocky, you wanted them to sit with you in your sadness
I trusted them with our family heirloom because I trusted you
And now you're both breaking
And I don't have the glue

So when the china set hit the ground with force
Scattering its remains across the floor
I knew you finally had enough
They thought you snapped that Thanksgiving
But I saw you emerge
Beyond the hands that provided care that created cracks
You had tears, but we knew how to take care of that

It was hard to see you hurt
Because there was nothing I could do
Finally after a while, you remembered you had wings
And this time I would help you follow through
Reminding you of the value of our family heirloom

ONE DAY

If you could give me just one more day to get it right
If you could give me one more day to release the loneliness
If you could give me one more day like...
Like when I first knew You were real
I promise to seek You enough to want to heal

But the days seemed colder this time around
And I don't know how I ended up in a space so dark
When all I've ever known You to be was light
I know you're there,
but it felt like you turned out the light in the room
forgetting I was sitting in the chair

I thought You forgot about me
So I decided to leave
And I never felt loneliness like this
Causing confusion about what I knew to be true
I searched and searched, screaming out for You

And when I realized You were the quiet in the storm, I exhaled
Being reminded of how You love me so
The darkness wasn't coming to attack me
You were reminding me to rest in Your presence

WHILE YOU WAIT

In this space between anticipation and receiving
The knowing, that You are guiding me through
It's the answers that I don't have
This is the waiting room
The place where most dreams die
And everyone being called on, except you, seems like the bad guy
The room where you let out your war cry
In hopes that you are being fortified
Because what else is there to do in the waiting room?
The place where you begin
Thinking about all of your sins
Wondering if your scars actually built you a thick skin
And then, your mind begins to spin
Uncontrollably
Asking 'How do we get out?'
'When will we hear from the doctor?'
And 'How much longer?'

All of these questions echo
the rhythm of my heart in desperation
Desperately wanting to get the cure
You opened the door and greeted me with an answer I didn't expect
When I asked 'What must you inject?'
You looked at me like I was perfect and didn't know it
While every fiber of my being said I was a reject

So I asked why I had to wait
And you retorted back to me
"What did you do while you waited?"
I was puzzled by the response
And the question because You already knew
You knew I cried
You knew I kept asking why
You knew I felt denied
And at that moment I knew,
The waiting room stole my hope

So your question wasn't because You didn't care
But it was for me to be built up again
So what do I do in the waiting room now?
I pray while I wait
I worship while I wait

I grow while I wait
I learn while I wait

Because when You call me in
I want to be restored fully
Laying the groundwork for what You've already promised me
So I don't mind the waiting room now
The waiting room is a promise
For that which I'll wait on

ASKING QUESTIONS PT. 1

How is your body feeling?
What about your mind?
Did you eat today?
Talk to me...

Did you go outside?
What is your favorite memory?
How can I support you?
Give yourself grace...

Do you feel lonely?
How can I make you feel safe?
Did joy find you today?
Breathe...

I'LL SEND YOU FLOWERS

I'll send you flowers
When the days seem darker
When you feel lonely at night
May each petal remind you of how beautiful you are when you bloom

I'll send you roses
Because roses show you love in its purest form
The thorns presently placed
As warning that you could get hurt,
But the softness of the petals remind you of your delicacy
So when you're roaming around wondering about your relevancy

I'll send you sunflowers
To remind you that you've always been my yellow
That you're the brightness that illuminates this life
And when it's all over, I promise to find you in paradise

I'll send you carnations
To show my admiration
For the strength you had even in isolation
Let it be a reminder to you
that your destiny is being fulfilled as you lay your foundation

I'll send you african violets
To remind you that God is inside you and everything else
And when you finally experience your breakthrough,
You'll be met with a wisdom that renews

So I promise on every 11/11 to send you flowers
When the days seem darker
When you feel lonely at night
May each petal remind you of how beautiful you are when you bloom

ASKING QUESTIONS PT. 2

Why don't I feel safe?
Why am I lonely?
What is going on?
What is in my control?

You told me to ask the questions
and now all of them are unanswered
I'm waiting for answers to show themselves
So my anxiety can take a backseat

But now the questions are taking a life of their own
Running around so fast
I barely have time to comprehend
What the question is

And this is where I sit
Day in and day out
Just asking questions
Wondering if in my questions
I'll finally learn to give myself grace

Maybe I'll stop worrying so much
Maybe I'll learn to quiet my thoughts
Maybe I'll be able to to breathe
Or maybe I'll still have more questions that go unanswered

But You told me to ask the questions
So that's what I'm doing
And I pray an answer or two find me
And when they do, I'm ready to accept

Was that what You were trying to teach me?
About the journey?
That I'll have to wait on the answers?
Thank You, for meeting me at my exit
I know how to get home from here.

THE LONG VERSION

I hope you know I want the long version of your truth
As you heal the trauma you didn't choose
I want the words that are held in the silence of your tears
Because I want you to breathe without any fear

I want the mundane version about your day
I want it to fill me in like you're writing an essay
And I'll help you walk with your emotions
In hopes that you feel my devotion - to you

I hope you know I want every version of you that emerges
And I'll celebrate with you as you find the key to your churches

I hope you know, I will bury the bodies of self doubt
And help you find roots in confidence on new ground

I hope you know, you're the interlude on my favorite record
And loving you isn't an exhaustive effort
Because to experience your love
Is a promise God fulfilled from above

So I always want the long version of your truth
And I'll even stay for the overflow too

DID YOU FIND JOY TODAY?

The last time I saw her, I was with you
Talking for hours about our plans
And I'm pretty sure she followed me home
But she never came in

I remember she showed up on my doorstep a few months ago
And it was a welcomed surprise
Chaos had finally settled in upstairs
But she could only stay for a day

Oh! I ran into her at the bookstore
We were walking down the aisles
Looking for a book we had been meaning to read
We sat at the cafe across the street and peace drove by

I can't remember the first time we met
But I have pictures from every time since
She came and watched a show with me
And we had a great night out at dinner
She even came back to my house
And we had a sleepover

For some reason, I haven't seen her in a while
I miss her presence
I flip through our photos
I wonder how she's doing
I wanted to call and catch up
But she's been busy lately

You heard she was back in town?
I'm sure we'll catch up soon

AUGUST 20

Dear Lord,
I ask that You expand my territory and continue to mold my virtues that they begin to match Yours. When I don't feel certain or close, may I quickly be reminded of how faithful You are. I want you to expand Your impact through me, beyond what I can understand; to guide more souls to Your kingdom. I ask that when I get to the gates, that I can be let in to see Your face and say 'Thank You" for guiding me. I ask that if You call me home sooner than my loved ones anticipated, that when I get to Your gates, I can give You a hug and help provide a spirit presence for my loved ones on Earth. I ask that You continue to guide me so that I seek Your wisdom, knowledge and understanding. I thank You for it all. Thank You for already doing it. I thank You for co-signing and partnering with me to fulfill my purpose. I honor You by honoring what I put in my body, mind and spirit.

In Jesus Name,
Amen.

LONELY'S HEARTBEAT

You came wrapped up like a gift
And I opened you unprepared
I thought I was on the train by myself
But I got to my seat and immediately felt your presence sit next to me
I thought you were waiting for someone else
And then panic hit
My head spinning against the shift
But my heart taking a moment to recalibrate to this new…rhythm

You looked at me with guilt in your eyes
And I wanted to ask you "Why?"
But my mouth was caught in a level of shock
I was just wondering if you had gotten lost

As I let my heart find a false sense of peace
My eyes were able to rest
When I got to my final destination
I woke up without you next to me
I thought maybe I had just been dreaming

But somehow you had already made yourself comfortable in my home
I looked around and couldn't recognize anything as my own
Everything was out of place
It felt as if you had rearranged it on purpose
Making me feel lost in my own safe space

You came in and flipped my world on its' axis
And you did it without remorse
Momma always said to mind your manners, so I let you stay
Because I'm not a bad host,
Thinking you had nowhere else to go
I wrapped around you and held you close
In hopes that joy could peak through
But when I woke up the next morning
I found you as just another pain in my shoe
I didn't know what else to do with you
I tried feeding you love
And that only made you sick
When I turned to my friends you started to tick
So I didn't understand why you couldn't just love me back
Why didn't you love me back?

It was the gritty feeling that puzzled me the most
I didn't understand why the space in my heart had to become your post
So when I talked to my therapist I was confused
Because you showed up one day without any cues
Determined to cause chaos in my mind
Pushing me into isolation that made me blind

I finally waited hoping that you would get the picture
So I could breathe again
Hoping you would leave again
But you never left

Your only motive was to cause more trouble
While I couldn't understand
I felt all of your demands
Of wanting to be the only thing I carried
Forcing me to dig up everything that I had buried

You disguised yourself as jealousy for a while
And I didn't understand because envy had never been my style
But then you…caressed me
You even dressed up nicely for the dinner parties
Put on a smile and let me laugh laugh for a while
But when the confetti had cleared
You let me know
You were always going to be right there

So I asked my therapist how do I kick you out? How do I let you go?
She reminded me about the night on the train
The night where you decided to take the reigns
The night you recalibrated my heart
The night you added a link to my chain of traumas
Leaving me with all of your bags full of karma
But this link wasn't like the other ones I've had before
No, because you entangled yourself in my heart this time
Changing the rhythm and beat of my own drum
Overwhelming me with all I had to confront

My therapist wondered why I never asked you your name
I thought I didn't have to because I never saw you as something to be gained
But she warned against me healing in vain
So there was no longer a cloak of anonymity attached to my pain

So when I came back home
And all the lights were off
I asked you "did you know how much you cost?"
You cost me my freedom to love
You cost me the clarity to seek
And you even cost me my friends and family
You turned and looked at me
Hoping that I would never let you go
And I yelled "You were never mine to keep!"

So you gave me back the key to my heart
To calibrate to the rhythm I knew
And I thanked you
But I still didn't know your name
So when you introduced yourself as lonely
I thought that's why I was in so much pain
You unlocked a new rhythm I never knew I had
I hated all the damage you caused
That made me go mad
But I wanted to say thank you
For introducing yourself to me
And no longer hiding behind the cloak of anonymity
Allowing me to expose a new rhythm of my heart
To ensure I do everything in my power, moving forward from letting it ever fall apart

DEAR Z

How do you say thank you to a person whose light was so bright?
How do you begin to repay how much they've impacted you?
The countless drives
The amount of times you would say, "Don't stay too long. Make sure you're resting."
I don't know what it means
When people remind you that every single day,
That those moments will now be the memories
The ones you collect over time
The ones where it makes your heart smile
The ones where you end up laughing more at the person's laugh than the moment itself
I didn't think I would have to do that with you
I didn't think that would be our story

See we assume that every moment will last forever
We assume that our strongest will be able to weather the storms that life presents
And every moment after
Yet no one prepared me for the moment after

The moment after I realized I couldn't call you
The moment after I realized the last time I saw your face was the last time
The moment after I realized you would never text me back
And never remind me to take a beat again
It's the moment after that breaks my heart
The moment after reminds me that the moments we were living are now just memories
And I don't want the memories
I wanted more opportunities
More chances to tell you I love you
Chances to hear you make fun of me
How dare you leave me
Leave me with the moments after that break my heart time and time again
Because the memory of you is now more painful than I can comprehend
How dare you leave me with the moments after
What happens when I don't remember your voice
Or keep replaying the time you told me to...
What happens in the moment after
What happens when the phone keeps ringing and no one picks up
See those are the moments you didn't prepare me for

See when we were living in our reality

I didn't understand that these would be the memories
The only ones I have left to hold onto
The only ones that distinctly remind me of you
I wasn't prepared, I wasn't ready
Because these weren't supposed to be the memories
The ones that tethered me to you for a lifetime
We were supposed to have a lifetime
But I'm grateful for each and every time
Reminding me to take a beat
Reminding me to laugh
Reminding me that it's not always that serious
We were supposed to have a lifetime
More opportunities to feel each other's presence with joy, peace
So the moment after you took up your wings
The moment after I had to say goodbye
The moment after I told you I loved you for the last time
I don't want to remember the moment after
I don't want to go towards the reality that waits after

So instead I'll say thank you
Thank you for the times you made the realities feel like bliss
Thank you for the times you made me laugh
Thank you for the times you saw my heart
Those are the times I will remember
Those will be the moments I carry
Those will be the moments I cherish
So I'll remind myself to take a beat
I'll remind myself that you loved me
I'll carry that with me, after this moment
Because it will pass
And the memories won't be so hard to remember

FIGHT BACK SEASON

This season came with hands
While laying in my abyss
Hoping that my pain would be dismissed

I didn't know how to offer myself grace
And the lies came in a stampede
Causing my weary eyes to bleed

But then you reminded me of the covenant
Allowing me to honor where I laid my head
But my reminding me that this layer must be shed

I want to give you grace for what you're feeling
But I also want to offer you it's fight back season
And even this storm has a greater reason

So put your gloves on and swing
With everything in you
Because the version you've prayed for is waiting to breakthrough

MEADOW

I had to to set the tone
Moving on my own
Into the territory unknown
And in the time that I've grown
You can finally see what I've sown

In the soil that was unforgiving
My roots remained in thanksgiving
Wondering if in my submitting
I'd end up losing

Losing the promise assigned to me
The promise of being free
Fighting to believe that your loyalty was guaranteed
So I pushed as if I had morphine

Flowing through my veins
While still plowing against the grain
So the seeds you planted in my pain
Became your weeds domain

But I was always destined to bloom
Like the four o'clocks under the moon
Enduring your illness with a great fortitude
I would finally see my promise come into view
Outgrowing what you tried to subdue
Instead of looking out
I had finally found my way through

Breaking through the soil that held despair
Finally breathing in fresh air
I didn't mind that this version had some wear and tear

I had landed in the place of my promise
So when I blossomed in my meadow
I felt the zenith of my promise begin to show
And my freedom...
well it overflowed like a rainbow

AFTERWORD

I want to say thank you God for meeting me at my exit. This is my first collection of poetry and this book has been a long time coming. I want to say thank you for taking the time to read, breathe and let these words have a life of their own. They aren't solely mine anymore, they are ours.

To my tribe of five, my biggest prayer is that the love and support you've given me during this journey may carry you to the abundant blessings assigned to you. I love each of you dearly and fiercely. I couldn't have done this without your steady hands, guidance, encouragement and love.

Thank you for journeying with me. If no one else tells you, I am telling you, you are divinely loved and worthy.

With Love,
K.M.

ABOUT THE AUTHOR

Keaton Mills

Follow Keaton Mills on social media:
Instagram: @keatonmills_
X (formerly Twitter): @keatonmills_
Tiktok: @keatonmills_

www.ingramcontent.com/pod-product-compliance
Lightning Source LLC
Chambersburg PA
CBHW051705040426
42446CB00009B/1314